Cutting the Children's Plan

A £5 billion experiment gone astray

TOM BURKARD AND TOM CLELFORD

THE AUTHORS

Tom Burkard is the Director of The Promethean Trust, a Norwich based charity for dyslexic children and the author of *Inside the Secret Garden: the progressive decay of liberal education* (University of Buckingham Press, 2007). He is the author of numerous influential reports for the Centre for Policy Studies on literacy, testing and school quangos; and is a member of the NAS/UWT and a Visiting Fellow at the University of Buckingham.

Tom Clelford is a free-lance researcher who is currently working for *The Spectator* and The Promethean Trust. He carried out a major portion of the research for the influential Centre for Policy Studies paper, *School Quangos: an agenda for abolition and reform*. He is also studying Politics at the University of East Anglia.

Acknowledgements
Support towards research for this Study was given by the Institute for Policy Research.

ISBN No. 978-1-906996-22-2

© Centre for Policy Studies, June 2010

Printed by 4 Print, 138 Molesey Avenue, Surrey

CONTENTS

A NOTE ON METHODOLOGY

In order make a reasonably accurate appraisal of what the Children's Plan costs the taxpayer, we have consulted information published by the DCSF, Department of Health and Home Office. These include press releases, white papers, guidance notes, and memoranda of grants. We have also consulted the websites of the quangos, charities and private companies involved in 'delivering' programmes; Hansard; National Statistics releases; and local authority circulars. Throughout the research underlying this report, we have found that the greatest difficulty is that officials have been unable (not necessarily unwilling) to give us the information that we needed.

Frequently, the sources were at odds, and in such cases we made Freedom of Information requests to the relevant body. Of the 19 requests we made, we received 15 responses, and we were able to obtain satisfactory figures in 17 instances. In some cases, we have had no option but to make estimates on the basis of the 2008-2011 CSR review.

Because of the difficulty in establishing the exact budgets of all the various aspects of the Children's Plan, it is inevitable that there will be some errors in this document. All numbers must therefore be treated with due caution.

SUMMARY

- The Children's Plan was published by the DCSF in December 2007. It consists of over 60 programmes and, in the words of the DCSF, "is a vision for change to make England the best place in the world for children and young people to grow up."

- The 2010-11 budget for the various elements in the Children's Plan is estimated at £5 billion a year (see Annex A, 2010-11 Funding by Programme).

- While it is true that social mobility and the opportunities of disadvantaged children are low, it is doubtful whether the programmes in the Children's Plan can ever achieve the high ambitions set out for them. Most are flawed both in concept and in practice.

- The following problems can be found in most programmes:

  – they are highly centralised, with regulations, "guidance on best practice" and funding all being controlled by the DCSF;

  – they are heavily influenced by prevailing educational and child-rearing orthodoxies;

- although intended to help those working with children, they are in practice likely to be highly bureaucratic;

- the implementation of programmes is left to a complex web of quangos, charities, private companies and local authorities, damaging transparency and accountability;

- evaluation of programmes has been criticised as weak by the House of Commons Health Select Committee.

- The most significant element (with a budget of £1.135 billion in 2010-11) of the Children's Plan is Sure Start. Originally designed to help the parents of the most disadvantaged children, this is now a network of 3,500 Children's Centres offering a wide range of services to all families in England.

- Evaluations of Sure Start have not always shown it to be a success (the first, in 2006, concluded that it had an adverse effect on the most deprived children in the country).

- An alternative approach, which can be applied to many of the more useful elements of the Children's Plan (including Sure Start), is to give local authorities the discretion to implement and fund these programmes.

- This approach would:

  - enable decisions to be taken at a local, not a national, level and improve accountability, innovation and further local involvement;

  - cut £1.9 billion a year (in terms of the 2010-11 budget) from the Children's Plan;

  - devolve responsibility for an additional £2.3 billion a year to local government;

  - leave £0.8 billion with central government.

SUMMARY OF RECOMMENDATIONS

£ millions	2010/11 Budget	Proposed central budget reduction
Programmes to support		
Extended Schools	£506	£280
Programmes to be devolved		
Sure Start and State funded Child Care	£2,317	£835
Aiming High for Disabled Children	£397	nil
PE and Sports Strategy for Young People	£191	£96
Programmes to abolish		
Early Years Foundation Stage	£315	£315
Food in Schools	£324	£414*
Youth Provision (Children's Plan)	£192	£162
National Challenge	£218	£218
Playgrounds, Playbuilders and Playworkers	£128	£9
Think Family	£65	£65
Every Child a Reader et al	£56	£56
Assessment for Learning etc	£65	£65
Special Educational Needs (Children's Plan)	£34	£34
Mental Health (TaMHS)	£28	£27
Safe at Home	£9	£9
Total devolved to local government	**£2,259 million**	
Total budget reduction	**£1,917 million**	

* For Food in Schools, the saving is greater than the 2010/11 budget as the actual cost of provision is estimated to be higher in future years.

1. INTRODUCTION

Large numbers of children in England start life at an extreme disadvantage. Parents who themselves may have been poorly educated are often incapable of giving their children experiences which foster intellectual and social growth. Many of these children live in estates where unemployment, crime, family breakdown, alcoholism and drug abuse are rife. For them, staying alive is a challenge: we should not be surprised that so few of them become educated and productive adults. And it is a sad fact that social mobility in the UK has remained static (at best) over the last 15 years with parental background remaining a much more significant determiner of children's life chances in the UK than elsewhere.[1]

What is the Children's Plan?

The Children's Plan, first published by the Department for Children, Schools and Families (DCSF)[2] in December 2007,

---

[1] See the recent report by John Ermisch and Emilia Del Bono, *Education Mobility in England – The link between the education levels of parents and the educational outcomes of teenagers*, Sutton Trust, 2010.

[2] The change of name of the DCSF to the Department of Education in May 2010 is welcome. However, for the sake of consistency, the Department is referred to throughout this report as the DCSF.

consists of a range of measures designed to equalise outcomes. It is nothing if not ambitious: in 2010-2011, it will cost £5 billion[3] – enough to fund eight additional teachers in every primary school in England.

The Children's Plan re-packaged and re-presented Every Child Matters (ECM),[4] along with a wide range of recent initiatives. In the words of the DCSF, the Children's Plan:[5]

> "...is a vision for change to make England the best place in the world for children and young people to grow up. It put the needs and wishes of families first, setting out clear steps to make every child matter".

Perhaps unintentionally, this statement reveals that the Children's Plan should be considered not so much as an integrated strategy as a (very expensive) public relations exercise for a broad range of new initiatives.

There are an estimated 66 funding streams of £1 million+ for 2010-11.[6] The 16 largest of these are considered in this report.[7]

---

[3] The 2010 Budget estimated that the total Department Expenditure Limit for the DCSF would be £51.5 billion in 2010/11. Note that the £5 billion cost of the Children's Plan does not take into account the burdens placed upon teachers and social workers, who often do not get compensated for additional duties they are required to assume as a result of the Children's Plan.

[4] ECM was launched in 2003 in response to Lord Laming's report into the Victoria Climbié scandal. Its intent was to improve the co-ordination of children's services.

[5] DCSF, *The Children's Plan*, 2007.

[6] See Appendix for a full list of these programmes with annual budgets £1 million.

[7] See Annex A for a list of programmes in the Children's Plan.

Some, such as the Extended Schools programme, may have real potential. Others, such as Sure Start or the School Food programme, have had little success in meeting their aims. Many elements do little more than duplicate or extend existing social and educational provision.

It may be argued that, if the measures in the Children's Plan were to improve significantly the lives of our most vulnerable children, then they would be a wise investment: the economic costs of maintaining an alienated underclass are enormous, and the human costs are incalculable.

Unfortunately, the outlook is not promising. Most of the ideas implemented in the Children's Plan have had little success in meeting their ambitious goals (and have already been tested to destruction in the US, where social divisions are still just as deep as when Lyndon Johnson launched his "War on Poverty" 46 years ago). If – as seems likely – the Children's Plan fares no better, we will simply have wasted a lot of money.

This is not to say that all the Children's Plan measures should be abandoned. As the Commons Health Committee has noted,[8] programme evaluation often amounts to little more than asking participants what they thought about all the money they had been given. It is hard to tell which aspects of the Children's Plan will have a lasting and positive impact.

This raises the question of who should make any decision on the future of these programmes. Should it be a government minister who decides whether, say, lunchbox inspections are necessary in Hampstead, Halifax or Haringey? Or should it be local families?

---

[8] House of Commons Health Select Committee, *Health Inequalities: Third Report of Session 2008–09*, February 2009.

3

For the centrally-led 'integrated delivery' model of the Children's Plan is hard to justify. The levels of inter- and intra-agency complexity undermines accountability and effectiveness. For instance, the Family Intervention Projects (FIPs) involve two government departments, 11 quangos, and countless charities and agencies in 150 local authorities. With so many bodies involved, responsibility is diffused to the point of invisibility. It is a wonder that any monies ever trickle down to the people that these programmes are meant to help.[9]

What is common to almost all programmes is their centralised and over-bureaucratic nature. Whitehall – or big government – is instructing local authorities, schools, playgroups, parents and other parts of civil society on how to bring up children.[10] We should not be surprised if the result is a heavy-handed, didactic approach inspired by whatever orthodoxy is currently in favour.

There is an alternative. A new Government, committed both to devolving power and to reducing quangos and bureaucracy, should reassess the underlying approach to the Children's Plan – and reform or abolish many of these expensive and ineffective programmes.[11] And this is in tune with the aims of the

---

[9]   The leaders of Westminster, Wandsworth and Hammersmith Councils have demonstrated how localisation works in practice. They estimate that £14 billion could be saved annually by the elimination of duplicated effort by various official bodies, quangos and third-sector organisations. See Colin Barrow et al, *A Magna Carta for Localism: Three practical steps to make localism real,* Centre for Policy Studies, March 2010.

[10] For an early analysis of the intrusive nature of centralised programmes such as Sure Start, see J Kirby, *The Nationalisation of Childhood,* Centre for Policy Studies, 2006.

[11] The 2010 Conservative manifesto pledged that "over the course of a Parliament, we will...save a further £1 billion a year from quango bureaucracy" and that "we need to push power down to the most appropriate local level: neighbourhood, community and local government". Similarly, the 2010 Liberal

"Big Society" programme launched by the Government in May 2010:[12]

"We want to give citizens, communities and local government the power and information they need to come together, solve the problems they face and build the Britain they want. We want society – the families, networks, neighbourhoods and communities that form the fabric of so much of our everyday lives – to be bigger and stronger than ever before. Only when people and communities are given more power and take more responsibility can we achieve fairness and opportunity for all."

In particular, responsibility for the potentially useful parts of the Children's Plan should be devolved to parents, schools and local authorities. It is they who can best decide which Children's Plan programmes are worthwhile; and for local government to administer and finance those that they wish to retain.[13]

Localisation of educational and social provision has already paid big dividends in Scotland, where two local authorities have all but wiped out illiteracy. The synthetic phonics programmes initiated by Dr Joyce Watson and Professor Rachel Johnston in Clackmannanshire and by Professor Tommy MacKay in West Dunbartonshire have virtually eliminated reading failure despite

---

Democrat manifesto pledged that "we will free schools from the present stranglehold of central government control and encourage them to be genuinely innovative" and named various education quangos for abolition.

[12] Cabinet Office, *Building the Big Society*, May 2010.

[13] It may be necessary to revise local authority funding formulae to take account of varying income and deprivation levels across the country.

the opposition of the education establishment.[14] Tellingly, these stunning achievements are ignored in the Children's Plan.

This report sets out which major elements of the Children's Plan are worthy of continuing support; which should be abolished; and which should be transferred to local authorities.

---

[14] See Tom Burkard, *A World First for West Dunbartonshire*, Centre for Policy Studies, 2006.

2. A GOOD IDEA: EXTENDED SCHOOLS

Many of England's schools open for fewer than 35 hours a week. The rest of the time classrooms and facilities for sport, drama, craft, technology and music are unused. Putting these facilities to work is one of the better ideas to emerge in the last dozen years. It has been enthusiastically endorsed by the Conservatives, who rightly recognise that one of the reasons why KIPP academies in the US are producing such amazing results with ghetto kids is their extended opening hours.[15]

Unfortunately, the present Extended Schools programme has not really taken off. Of the announced revenue funding of £476 million for 2010-11, about £50 million has not been taken up.[16] As

---

[15] In the US, there are now 82 KIPP academies serving over 21,000 children – 90% of them are eligible for free school meals, and 95% are black or Hispanic. KIPP schools ignore this putative 'disadvantage', and teach all children a demanding curriculum. This positive approach pays huge dividends: 85% of KIPP pupils go on to higher education.

[16] Announced Extended Schools Subsidy for 2010-11 was £217 million (DCSF press notice 2007/0126, 10 July 2007, *Building on Achievement, Meeting New Challenges*). Actual allocation in 2010-11 was £167 million (DCSF, 2010, Standards Fund Allocations 2008-2011). Total allocated Extended Schools funding for 2010-2011 is £460 million.

with other Children's Plan initiatives, it has been stunted by excessive bureaucracy. It is unrealistic to expect heads and teachers to take on additional duties at all when they are already so weighed down by central government demands.

What are Extended Schools?

Extended Schools, or Full Service Extended Schools, were first introduced in 2003 by DfES. The 2005 Extended Schools Prospectus sets the goal that all schools will provide access to the 'core offer' by 2010; currently around two thirds do so. The 'core offer' consists of five parts:

- childcare (8am-6pm, 48 weeks a year for primary schools and special schools);

- a varied menu of activities (including study support, play/recreation, sport, music, arts and crafts and other special interest clubs, volunteering and business and enterprise activities), in a safe place, for primary and secondary schools;

- swift and easy access to targeted and specialist services such as speech and language therapy;

- parenting support including family learning; and

- community access to facilities including adult and family learning, ICT and sports facilities.

An important word to note in the mandate for Extended Schools is 'access'. The schools do not have to provide all the services themselves. If the service in question is provided nearby, then the school can direct people to it. Also important is the caveat in the small print which says if there is no local demand for a particular service, it does not need to be provided.

The potential for Extended Schools

The potential of this idea can easily be judged by comparing the existing adult evening courses for teaching a foreign language with GCSE French and German lessons taught in secondary schools. The former are eagerly attended by people who are willing to pay to learn, and expect to learn. When teachers don't deliver, their courses will be under-subscribed, and soon be dropped. By contrast, the sole aim of school languages is to get a qualification. Teachers are forced to adopt ever more unreal tactics to get their pupils to pass the arcane criteria set by officials.[17] Giving pupils a chance to attend evening courses in addition to their GCSE lessons would give them the opportunity to study a language for its own sake, sitting alongside motivated adults. This would, in all probability, prove a resounding success.

Extended Schools could also play a key role in the education of gifted pupils. Good teachers would welcome the chance to work with pupils who are both motivated and able. Remedial classes for the least able could also prevent pupils from falling so far behind that they are incapable of engaging the curriculum at any level. Local colleges would no doubt be keen to offer both vocational and academic courses for pupils with the appropriate aptitude and ability.

Extended schools could also do much to broaden the range of extra-curricular sporting and cultural activities currently available for pupils in state schools (particularly secondary schools). Pupils can benefit greatly when schools stay open for

---

[17] Warwick Mansell has explained that, in order to pass GCSEs, many average pupils are encouraged merely to learn to recite simple passages by heart. See *Education by numbers*, Politico's, 2007.

longer (particularly when the range of local alternatives is limited).[18]

The Budget for Extended Schools

(£ million)	2008-2009	2009-2010	2010-2011
Revenue Funding			
Extended Schools Start up	£97	£172	£71
Sustainability Funding	£74	£135	£190
Extended Schools Subsidy	£7	£38	£167
Academic Focused Study Support	£0	£34	£33
Capital Funding			
Extended Schools Capital Funding	£84	£89	£46
Total	**£261**	**£467**	**£506**

Sources: See Annex A.

Seven recommendations

The Extended Schools Programme clearly has great potential. If this potential is to be unleashed then the following changes are required:

1. Teachers should be paid fairly for additional hours worked. Participation should be optional, and heads should be free to engage the most effective teachers.

2. Extended Schools will only work effectively if the bureaucratic burden imposed by central government on teachers is substantially reduced. It is unrealistic, for example, to expect teachers to function effectively after hours if they are also expected to 'personalise' learning for all of their pupils.

---

[18] For an analysis of why the range of activites available in schools needs to be broadened, see Anthony Seldon, *An End to Factory Schools*, Centre for Policy Studies, 2010.

3.	In addition to classes conducted by school staff and aimed exclusively at its pupils, schools should be free to organise whatever activities are desired by pupils, parents and other local people, and to bring in outsiders to teach and organise them. Adult evening classes should be encouraged wherever possible, with classes opened to pupils and other young people where appropriate. Schools should be free to negotiate fees for the use of their facilities and allowed to keep the revenue generated from such activities.

4.	Primary funding should be locally raised from a combination of public and private sources, fees and parental contributions. A degree of matching central funding is also necessary, adjusted for the level of local needs.

5.	As the Association of Teachers and Lecturers recommends, the Independent Safeguarding Authority should be scrapped (saving £8 million a year).

6.	The draconian nature of Health and Safety guidelines should be revised. Enthusiasm for new ideas drains quickly when those involved have to conduct over-burdensome risk assessments.

7.	The Core Offer should be dropped. Schools should have the freedom to decide whether or not they provide extended services.

Clearly, not all schools will want to participate in the Extended Schools programme, and this should be a matter for parents, staff and school governors to decide. But the example of those schools which do have the initiative and drive to try new ideas should lead to widespread use over time.

Estimated impact on central funding

The central government budget for Extended Schools should be reduced to reflect the actual usage in 2010/11. This would cut £50 million from central government funding relative to original allocations.

In addition, those schools which wish to participate should be expected to raise a proportion of funds locally, either through local authority funding or through their own fund-raising activities. Funds raised should be topped up with matching central funding set at a level to reflect the level of need in a school's catchment area.[19] Assuming that, on average, local fund-raising would equal that of central government, central funding would fall from £460 million to £230 million a year.

---

[19] Spot auditing of accounts would be needed to prevent abuse.

3. A BAD IDEA: SURE START

Sure Start has its origins in the 1998 Green Paper *Meeting the Childcare Challenge*, which announced the creation of 25 'Early Excellence centres.' Its aim was to give "children the best possible start in life" through improvement of childcare, early education, health and family support, with an emphasis on outreach and community development. The programme was originally intended to support disadvantaged families in areas of above average deprivation from pregnancy until children were four years old. Following Every Child Matters in 2005,[20] it now covers all families with children up to age 14 (or 16 for those with disabilities). Total revenue funding in this financial year is £1.55 billion.[21] Note that in this section, we have separated funding for Sure Start and state-funded childcare. In practice the two are closely intertwined but the distinction can help to highlight the potential for savings.

---

[20] Every Child Matters, or ECM for short, is the government initiative on child care that was launched in 2003, at least partly in response to the death of Victoria Climbié.

[21] DCSF, *Sure Start, Early Years and Childcare grant and Aiming High for Disabled Children Allocations Table 2008 – 2011*, 2010/11.

Sure Start is now delivered through a network of 3,500 Children's Centres in England.[22] These Children's Centres are now required to offer a huge range of well-meaning (but highly statist) services including:

- Information and advice to carers on a range of subjects, including local childcare, early years provision and education services for three and four-year olds

- Outreach services for isolated parents/carers and children at risk of social exclusion

- Links to local schools and out-of-school activities

- A system in place to provide early identification of children with special needs and disabilities

- A programme of activities designed to increase families' understanding of child development and to raise parenting skills

- A programme of activities to raise community awareness, promote community cohesion and foster positive relations between different communities

- Information, guidance and support on breastfeeding, nutrition, hygiene, healthy lifestyles, safety and smoking cessation

- Arrangements for consulting parents and ensuring that their views and needs are taken into account when planning and delivering service

---

[22] The number of Children's Centres was derived from a DCSF response to a Freedom of Information request, 19 January 2010.

State Funded Childcare

The Childcare Act 2006 imposed on Local Authorities the duty to secure sufficient childcare to enable parents to take up work or training, and the duty to provide the proscribed early years childcare free of charge. It also required all childminders to sign up to the childcare register, held by Ofsted; and also required all registered early years childminders to comply with the Early Years Foundation Stage.

In January 2009, the New Opportunities White Paper stated the Labour Government's long-term "goal of extending free early learning and childcare places to all two-year olds."

From September 2009 every LA in the country has offered 15% of their most disadvantaged 2 year olds either 10 or 15 hours of childcare 38 weeks a year. In 2010-2011 this will cost £67 million. If this service were provided in 2010-2011 to every child in the country (as stated in the New Opportunities White Paper), even at the lowest tier of funding (£4.85 per hour for 10 hours per week) the cost would be £1.31 billion.[23]

Evaluations of Sure Start

The first evaluation of Sure Start in 2006 concluded that it had an adverse effect on the most deprived children. It suggested that:[24]

> "...because the most socially deprived groups account disproportionately for many problems in

---

[23] See www.dcsf.gov.uk/everychildmatters/_download/?id=6174 for data on costs etc. Rising birth rates would push costs even higher; 2008 saw the most births in England since 1972. DCSF's projections for the cost of the provision were based on 600,000 2 year olds; in 2008, 708,708 children were born. See ONS, *Population Trends – Winter 2009*, 2009.

[24] J Belsky et al, "Effects of Sure Start local programmes on children and families", *BMJ*, 2006.

society (such as school problems and crime), the apparent adverse effects of [Sure Start Local Programmes] might have greater consequences for society than the beneficial effects."

At that stage, it was reported that Tony Blair was ready to cancel the initiative, but that Gordon Brown intevened to save it. David Cameron's original position was guarded: although he supported the principle of early intervention, he was careful not to endorse the programme itself. In 2006, Channel 4 News reported his comments:

"I'm a big fan of the thinking behind Sure Start. It's during the very early years that children from deprived backgrounds lose out most, and it's here that parents most need support."

He was careful not to attack Sure Start in his own words, quoting instead a parent from Wythenshawe, who described the project as "a complete and utter waste of three million quid".

A further evaluation of Sure Start was conducted in 2008 and was more favourable. But there is still very little evidence that it is achieving its initial aim of improving the social and cognitive skills of disadvantaged children.[25] Gains were noted in only five of the 14 measures monitored. And over this period, if teaching

---

[25] After Sir Michael Rutter, one of Britain's most respected authorities on school effectiveness studies, served as an adviser for the evaluation of the Sure Start programme, he stated: "Why, we may ask, did the Government rule out any form of randomised controlled trials design, given its superior strength for determining efficacy? It may be presumed that the reason was political... [such trials would] carry the danger of showing that a key policy was a mistake." "Labour's Child Poverty Drive is Flawed, Says its own Adviser", *Sunday Telegraph*, 16 September 2006.

unions are to be believed, even more children are coming to school with severe behavioural disorders.

The broadening of the original remit of Sure Start has raised concerns. For example, in 2008, the House of Commons Health Select Committee remarked that:[26]

"Sure Start programmes were being 'colonised' by the middle classes, who enjoyed the cheap, high quality childcare they offer and that extending provision universally would further dilute their focus on those who need them the most."

The report continues that the then Health Secretary Alan Johnson did not think this was a problem, but "he did not give us a clear explanation of why the policy was being extended". The report continues:

"...there is concern that extending this policy, via Children's Centres, to all areas of the country, risks distracting from the original focus of deprived families who are most in need of support. We did not receive detailed evidence about the evolution of Sure Start programmes into Children's Centres, but again this is a policy change that has not been properly piloted or evaluated prior to its introduction. It is absolutely essential that early years interventions remain focused on those children living in the most deprived circumstances, and Children's Centres must be rigorously monitored on an ongoing basis."

---

[26] www.publications.parliament.uk/pa/cm200809/cmselect/cmhealth/286/286.pdf

The Budget for Sure Start

£ millions	2008-09	2009-10	2010-11
Revenue	£885	£1,023 million	£1,135 million
Capital	£376 million	£552 million	£415 million
Total	**£1,261 million**	**£1,575 million**	**£1,551 million**

Sources: See Annex A.

Without reform, the Sure Start budget will grow substantially. The number of young children is rising fast with the birth rate hitting a 25 year high in 2008.[27]

In addition, the budget for Childcare is esimated at £767 million in 2010-11.

Recommendations

The Coalition proposals are, at this stage, open to a variety of interpretations. They have pledged to protect Sure Start from cuts and, although they "support the provision of free nursery care for pre-school children", they intend to "take Sure Start back to its original purpose of early intervention, [and] increase its focus on the neediest families".

Since they also intend "to pay for 4,200 extra Sure Start health visitors", it would appear that Coalition is actually proposing to increase Sure Start funding. This would certainly be the case if free nursery care is to be provided for all children, including those under the age of three.

An alternative would be that all Sure Start centres should become self-funding. These Centres should however be allowed to apply for grants (of say £1,000 per pupil per year) to pay for

---

[27] ONS, *Population Trends – Winter 2009*, 2009.

'at-risk' children, as defined by agreed criteria.[28] Grants would be administered by the local authority at their own expense, and Sure Start Centres would be spot checked to prevent abuse. This approach would be in keeping with the spirit of localisation.

Estimated impact on central funding

The following factors render any estimate of savings as highly problematic:

- There is no central data on the number of children now using Sure Start, so it is impossible to calculate the cost per child.

- It is difficult to say how many parents of at-risk children would come forward for Sure Start. Parents with mental illnesses or drug or alcohol problems are the least likely to attend, and of course these are the ones most likely to have problems.

- At-risk children will be more likely to require expensive specialist intervention.

- It would not be possible to close 90% of all Sure Start centres without stranding a substantial number of at-risk children. Reducing the numbers of children at each centre would not reduce fixed overheads.

However, efforts could be focussed on the 10% of poorest famlies with pre-school children. This would involve approximately 300,000 families. If Sure Start Centres were to receive grants to cover these families (as proposed above), the annual cost would be reduced to £300 million, yielding savings of £835 million.

---

[28] That level of funding is twice the current per pupil funding calculated for an authority such as Barnsley.

4. PROGRAMMES FOR DEVOLVING TO LOCAL AUTHORITIES

Aiming High For Disabled Children

This programme is intended to help the parents of disabled children through respite care for parents and other support services.

The provision of help for carers of disabled children is undeniably beneficial to both parties. Many parents make great sacrifices to keep children at home, and they should be supported and encouraged to do so. When parents give up and put their children in care, the cost to the taxpayer is considerable, and the welfare of the child is often severely compromised. It is traumatic enough for any child to go into care – and it can only be worse for a child with severe disabilities (10% of children in care have disabilities compared to 5% of the total population).[29]

---

[29] Children in Need data, DfES and Family Resource Survey, DWP, 2004-5 cited in HM Treasury and DfES, *Aiming High for Disabled Children: Better Support for Families*, 2007.

The budget is £397 million in 2010/11, of which £229 million is on Short Break Services (respite care).[30] Funding involves the DCSF and the Department of Health, and it is administered by local authorities, NHS Primary Care Trusts, a private contractor (Serco), The Family Fund, Together for Children and Contact a Family.

The present arrangements are questionable. For parents, the process of applying for help is extremely complex and stressful. David Cameron has proposed that the existing arrangements be simplified, with only one organisation involved – an idea supported by Scope, the leading charity for disabled people.[31]

Individual Budgets
An interesting scheme that is being developed under this programme is the piloting of Individual Budgets (IB).[32] Six IB pilots began in April 2009 and are providing families with funding directly so that they can use it to best fulfil their individual needs. These pilots will receive between £200,000 and £280,000 funding from April 2009 to March 2011.[33] The Coalition programme also indicates that the new Government "will extend the greater roll-out of personal budgets to give people and their carers more control and purchasing power" and that it will "use direct payments to carers and better

---

[30] DCSF, 2010, SSEYCG and AHDC Allocations 2008-11; DOH funding to Primary Care Trusts for 2010-11 estimated at £113 million from comprehensive spending review allocations.

[31] http://news.bbc.co.uk/1/hi/uk_politics/8153116.stm

[32] This concept was first developed in a Centre for Policy Studies report by Florence Heath and Richard Smith (*People, not budgets: valuing disabled children*, CPS, 2004).

[33] Total Individual Budgets funding– 2009-2010: £713,631; 2010-11: £753,110 – DCSF, 2010, SSEYCG and AHDC Allocations 2008-11.

community-based provision to improve access to respite care".[34]

Recommendation
Currently, funding is disbursed through various third-sector organisations to approved providers of respite care. We suggest that the current level of funding be maintained, but that it be disbursed directly to parents and carers to use as they see fit. Local authorities should be responsible for administration, the cost of which they should bear. Local charities and voluntary organisations should also be encouraged to respond to the needs of this sector.

The Individual Budget trials should be closely monitored and rolled out nationally as and when they are successfully established.

Estimated impact on central funding
This proposal would not involve any change in the total spent on helping disabled children. It would however eliminate much of the bureaucracy and waste involved in the current scheme.

The PE and Sports Strategy for Young People
The DCSF estimate that, in 2002, only 25% of children participated in two hours of "high quality" PE every week.[35] The Children's Plan reported that this had increased to 86% by 2007 and announced the government's intentions to:[36]

> "...ensure that by 2011 all 5 to 16-year-olds also have the opportunity to participate in an additional three hours of sporting activity either within or outside

---

[34] HM Government, *The Coalition: our programe for government*, May 2010.

[35] DCSF and DCMS, *PE & Sports Strategy for Young People*, 2008.

[36] *Children's Plan*, page 75.

school; and that this three hour offer also applies to young people aged 16–19."

In 2008, the PE and Sports Strategy for Young People (PESSYP) promised "at least £755 million" to achieve these goals.[37] The school element of the strategy was setting up and centrally funding 450 'School Sports Partnerships'. These were networks of schools clustered around Sports Colleges.

The DCSF could not confirm funding for 2010-11. However based on previous years' funding it is likely to be around £155 million. Of this, around £136 million goes to schools; £5 million is spent on FE school sports coordinators and £15 million is spent maintaining the Youth Sport Trust, a charity whose chief purpose is to support school sports partnerships.[38] In addition, £13 million is allocated to Playing for Success,[39] a scheme which aims to motivate pupils at risk of falling behind in core subjects by holding catch up sessions in sports venues, for example football grounds. Funds are matched by the LA and the venue.

The quango Sport England is also running the 'Sport Unlimited' programme with a three year budget of £36 million. Sport Unlimited offers children 10 week tasters in different sports in the hope that they will continue once the taster is over. Over 90 'sports' are eligible for funding, including playing the Nintendo Wii.[40] Sport England's costs are likely to be higher; they spent £22.7 million on the PESSYP in 2008-2009.[41]

---

[37] DCSF and DCMS, *PE & Sports Strategy for Young People*, 2008.

[38] Freedom of Information response from DCSF, 13 May 2010.

[39] DCSF, *Standards Fund Allocations 2010-11*, 2010.

[40] *The Times*, 2 August 2009.

[41] House of Commons Written Answers, 9 June 2009.

It should be noted that, despite huge increases in funding, participation in sport has decreased since 1987. In 1987, 61% of adults engaged in at least one sporting activity in the four weeks preceding their interview.[42] This fell to 53.6% in 2007-2008.[43] Sport England's Taking Part Child Survey shows no statistically significant change in sports participation for the 11 to 16 year olds between 2006 and 2007.

Recommendation
The failure of central funding to increase participation indicates that a more effective alternative would be to disburse all central funds directly to schools, who should be free to use this money as they see fit on sporting activities for their pupils.

Estimated impact on central funding
This proposal would eliminate much of the bureaucracy and waste involved in the current scheme. By abolishing sports partnerships we estimate that the amount of central funding could be reduced by around £61 million without affecting front line services.[44] Abandoning Sport England's element of the PESSYP and the Playing for Success scheme could save another £35 million annually.

---

[42] Trends in Participation in Sports – National Statistics.

[43] DCMS, *Taking Part: The National Survey of Culture, Leisure and Sport.*

[44] Competition managers cost £9 million in 2009-2010 (Freedom of Information Response from DCSF, 13 May 2010); Partnership development managers cost around £16 million (advertised wage of £35,000 x 450 Sports Partnerships); the 900 specialist link teachers cost around £21 million (based on average teacher's salary of £23,000: Office of National Statistics, 2009, Annual Survey of Hours and Earnings); and DCSF funding to the Youth Sports Trust was £15 million in 2009-2010.

5. PROGRAMMES FOR ABOLITION

The Early Years Foundations Stage (EYFS)

The EYFS, which was launched in March 2007, had a budget of £315 million in 2010/11.[45] It was inspired by the laudable aim of ensuring that all infants enjoy a humane and stimulating childhood. Its aim is:[46]

> "...to help young children achieve the five Every Child Matters outcomes of staying safe, being healthy, enjoying and achieving, making a positive contribution, and achieving economic well-being."

The primary function of EYFS is to develop the standards and qualifications of all those in the childcare industry up to age five . This includes teachers and teaching assistants in reception yearat primary schols, and all nursery school staff (whether private or public sector) and childminders. EYFS Statutory Framework explains how this is to be achieved, describing different practices which the EYFS practitioner should be following to fulfil the ECM

---

[45] DCSF, 2010, SSEYCG and AHDC grant allocations 2008-2011.

[46] 4Children, *The Early Years Foundation Stage and out of school provision,* 2008.

outcomes. It lists a set of Welfare Requirements and a set of Learning and Development (L&D) Requirements, which must be followed by all providers of care for pre-school children (i.e. those below five years old).[47]

In addition, all childcare providers, including childminders, nurseries, kindergartens and pre-school classes, are obliged to register in order to operate legally. To become and remain registered they must comply with the Welfare requirements, and with the L&D requirements for settings in England.

These Learning and Development requirements are unusual in principle in imposing compulsory educational targets for children below the age of compulsory education, and on providers outside the state system and not receiving state funding.

This was a highly intrusive attempt for the state to micro-manage all pre-school childcare. The attempt to dictate 'best practice' to every parent, childminder and teacher in England is surely misguided (at best). As in any other area of human activity, there are many different ways to do things, and it is this very diversity that stimulates progress.

And it is questionable whether EYFS does indeed encourage good practice. For example, in reading, Reception Year children now do 'pre-reading' activities instead of learning to read through synthetic phonics (Ruth Miskin has shown that disadvantaged children are capable of getting a head start in reading long before their fifth birthday[48]). As a result, children from less stimulating environments waste an entire year, falling

---

[47] This requirement was created by the Childcare Act 2006.

[48] T Burkard, *The End of Illiteracy? The Holy Grail of Clackmannanshire,* Centre for Policy Studies, 1998.

even further behind their middle-class peers, whose parents generally know better than to delay reading instruction.

Despite the ambitions of the EYFS, it is unlikely that it has had much practical effect on the nation's childminders, other than the creation of more bureaucracy and paperwork. On one forum, a woman named Mishmash (who has an "outstanding Ofsted report") describes its limited impact in the real world:[49]

> "All you have to do really is take photos of children doing activities or something new, and put it into a little personal book for them. For example, when you take your six year old going to the park take a photo of him/her playing on the equipment and write underneath the photo the link to the six learning areas."

Recommendation and implication for funding
The EYFS should be scrapped. This would save £315 million a year.

Food in Schools

The Children's Plan included provisions for improving the quality of school food and piloting the extension of free school meal provision. The 2009 Pre-Budget Report made further commitments in this area; in 2010-2011 £45 million is budgeted to be spent on piloting some form of extended Free School Meals (FSM) provision to pupils whose parents are not in receipt of means-tested benefits.[50] The total cost of all school food

---

[49] See Sure Start forum at www.dcsf.gov.uk/forums/fusetalk/surestart/

[50] £10 million was allocated to extended free school meal pilots in 2010-2011 with matched funding from participating LAs: DCSF, "New £20m Free School Meals Pilot", press notice 2008/0212. 2008. A further £35 million was allocated in HM Treasury, *Pre-Budget Report 2009*, 2009.

measures is £324 million in 2010-2011.[51] The intention of these measures is to de-stigmatise FSM, and to promote 'healthy eating'.

There is little evidence that the aims are being met. The School Food Trust (SFT) – the quango set up in 2005 to administer the programme – itself admitted that "nutrient-based standards prove too difficult to implement in secondary schools resulting in non-compliance."[52] Take-up of school meals is only 39.3% in primary schools and 35.1% in secondary schools. The SFT itself suggests that there has only been a 0.1% increase in primary take-up and a 0.5% increase in secondary schools.[53]

Voices from within the catering industry confirm this. Geoffrey Harrison, managing director of one of the few catering services who bucked the trend of falling uptake (warns that "People are looking for easy answers by introducing nutritional standards – but it won't be the quick fix they hope."[54] Harrison's misgivings are expanded by the commentary from the 2007 Local Authority Catering Association (LACA) survey:[55]

---

[51]   This is comprised of £45 million to pilot FSM (see above); £140 million for the 50% funding of raise in FSM threshold (HM Treasury, *Pre-Budget Report 2009*, 2009). £79 million for the School meal subsidy (DCSF, *Standards Fund Allocations 2008-2011*, 2010); £7.7 million for School Food Trust funding (Stamford, 26th May 2010, Government Slashes School food Trust's budget by £1m, Caterersearch.com news); £50 million for School Kitchen Capital funding (targeted capital fund for kitchens and dining rooms, estimate based on 2 year allocation) £2.5 million for cooking ingredients for FSM pupils (DCSF press notice 2008/0015, 22 January 2008, Compulsory cooking lessons for all young people).

[52]   SFT, Financial Statements 2008.

[53]   SOURCE DETAILS.

[54]   Catersearch.com, 24, August 2006.

[55]   www.warrington.gov.uk/images/LACASurvey2007_tcm15-20615.pdf

"...believe that such radical changes to young people's dietary habits are too draconian and the speed of their introduction is too fast. LACA cannot expect to reverse an embedded eating culture nor can we expect to convert teenagers to a healthier regime by force overnight."

The DCSF allocated £10 million in 2010-11 to fund three pilot projects on extending FSMs. The pilot LAs match the central funding and two (Newham and Durham) are providing universal FSMs. The third, Wolverhampton, was trialling extending the FSM provision to children from families who have an annual income of up to £16,040. This pilot has been superseded by a commitment in the 2009 Pre Budget Report to extend free school meal eligibility to children whose parents receive working tax credit and have an annual income of up to £16,190. The expansion will cost £280 million a year, but only 50% of the funding was released in 2010-11.[56]

The 2009 Pre Budget Report also promised an additional £35 million to fund a universal FSM pilot in each region of the country in 2010-2011. The aim of the pilots is "to undertake a robust, independent, evaluation on the health and other benefits, in order to come to a view about the value for money of extending FSMs."[57] If FSMs were indeed extended to all pupils, then the following table shows how the annual costs would be around £2.7 billion:

---

[56] HM Treasury, *Pre Budget Report 2009*, 2009.

[57] www.teachernet.gov.uk/educationoverview/currentstrategy/freemealsandtrips/

	FTE Pupils	Individual meal	Daily Cost	Annual Cost
Primary	3,945,080	£1.91	£7.5 million	£1.4 billion
Secondary	3,270,760	£2.01	£6.6 million	£1.2 billion
Special	89,260	£1.94	£0.2 million	£0.03 million
TOTAL	7,305,100	n/a	£14,288,339	£2.7 billion

Notes: Data on number of FTE pupils from DCSF, *Schools Pupils and Their Characteristics*, January 2009. Part time pupils are counted as 0.5 FTE. Average cost per meal from the Third School Food Trust Survey, 2007 LACA Survey. Annual cost assumes 190 school days.

Note that around 250,000 children do not take up their entitlement to free school meals.[58]

Recommendation

Although the concern for children's health is understandable, the question is whether children's menus are best decided by a quango; or by people with a genuine stake in the outcome: their parents and teachers.

The latter is preferable. Schools' governing bodies should therefore be given autonomy over their food policy (if any) and their choice of caterers. Central involvement should be limited to provision of a free, optional template for contracts. Tender for these contracts should be open to anyone with the appropriate food safety qualifications – restricting tenders to 'approved' providers restricts competition. School food subsidies for needy children should be ring-fenced and given directly to schools. The expansion of the FSM threshold should be abandoned.

---

[58] Nelson et al, *National Indicator 52 Take up of school lunches in England 2008-2009*, School Food Trust, 2009. Comparison with previous years is impossible due to significant changes in methodology.

Estimated impact on central funding

Abolition of the Food in Schools programme would save £414 million a year.[59]

Children's Plan Youth Provision

Youth Provision is intended to provide out-of-school activities for young people. There is little evidence to support the belief that anti-social behaviour can be reduced by the provision of wholesome alternative activities. However desirable it may be to have youth centres where young people can gather and indulge in lawful activity, this is rightly the sort of project which should originate in the community, or be supplied by private enterprise. The budget in 2010-11 to improve youth facilities was £192 million, of which revenue funding is £135 million.

The largest element is Funding for Positive Activities for Young People (PAYP) with £94.5 million for the current year.[60] PAYP projects recruit 'key workers' who engage 'at-risk' youth during school holidays. In the local authorities where PAYP was piloted, it proved difficult to recruit and retain key workers, which indicates that the programme is not really viable. In any case, funds pass through five layers of bureaucracy before it reachers the activity providers.[61]

---

[59] The majority (£280 million) of this saving will be made by reversing the expansion of the FSM threshold. The remainder is made up of the various revenue streams of the school food programme cited above. Capital funding for school kitchens is not due to continue.

[60] DCSF, *Local Authority children's services funding worksheet 2008-2011*, 2007.

[61] The project is overseen nationally by an Operations Management Group (OMG), responsible for overall management and authoring guidance. The Regional Co-ordination Unit (RCU) is responsible for monitoring and co-ordinating the relationship with the Government Offices. Government offices have regional managers in place who are responsible for delivering PAYP within their area and manage the contracts with Lead Delivery Agents (LDAs).

The Youth Opportunity Fund and the Youth Capital Fund are projects intended to involve young people in the planning and commissioning of youth facilities. Unfortunately, this does not seem to have been effective; in the areas surveyed for the project evaluation less than half of the young people interviewed agreed that facilities had improved.[62] Funding for the current year is £67 million.[63]

Myplace is a programme which provided capital to start youth clubs. All funding has already been awarded, and the clubs are expected to generate their own revenue to fund operating costs. There are no cost implications beyond 2010-2011.

Recommendation and estimated impact on central funding
All central funding should be withdrawn. This would save £162 million a year.

National Challenge
The National Challenge started in June 2008 after trials in London, the Black Country and Manchester. Schools are eligible for National Challenge Funding if less than 30% of their pupils are achieving five A*-C grades at GCSE.

The budget for the National Challenge in 2010/11 is projected to be £217 million.[64] Much of this funding will be spent on "a small

---

There are 52 LDAs including Connexions and Youth Offending Teams (YOTs), some of whom work directly with activity providers and some of whom have another layer of management, Local Delivery Partners (LDPs), between them.

[62] See Golden et al, *Outcomes of the Youth Opportunity Fund/Youth Capital Fund, National Foundation for Educational Research*, 2008.

[63] DCSF, *Youth Opportunity Fund and Youth Capital Funds 2010-2011*, 2010.

[64] Freedom of Information response from the DCSF, 29 April 2010.

army of advisers" (who are said to be being paid £1,000 for every day they work with a school).[65]

At first sight, the programme has been a great success: the number of schools failing to achieve this goal has dropped from around 1,600 to 247 since New Labour came into office.[66] But, as Tony Gardiner – a senior maths lecturer at the University of Birmingham – has noted, when dealing with large samples, improvements of this order are mathematically impossible to achieve in such a short time span.

As a result of the National Challenge, the targeted secondary schools have been encouraged to concentrate their efforts on pupils who are just below the threshold, which inevitably leads to the neglect of both the most and least able pupils. In order to ensure a minimum C-grade, teachers are said to drill pupils in formulaic responses which often have little reflection on subject mastery.

Even worse, the National Challenge incentivises schools to find the easier alternatives – and exam boards and the Government are only too happy to provide them. One science teacher has said that schools were increasingly using BTEC awards (equivalent to two GCSEs), because most of them consist of only coursework. But since pupils know that the award is more important to the school than it is to them, they generally expect teachers to do most of the coursework for them. The head of a top Norwich comprehensive has said that their position in the

---

[65] "Army surplus: the government has announced yet another layer of advisers to be flown in to underperforming schools. But how helpful are they?", *The Guardian*, 18 November 2008.

[66] DCSF, press notice 2010/0014, *New figures show further improvements in secondary schools in England*, 2010.

league tables suffered because he refused to use the easier exam boards.[67]

Recommendation and estimated impact on central funding
The National Challenge has distorted teachers' priorities in order to meet an artificial benchmark. The Pupil Premium proposed by the current Coaltion Government is likely to be a far more effective method of helping schools in disadvantaged areas. The National Challenge should be abolished at a saving of £217 million a year.

Playgrounds – Pathfinders, Playbuilders, and Playworkers
The Children's Plan and the National Play Strategy set out the DCSF's plans for children's play and the means to implementing them. It is an ongoing project with targets, albeit vague ones, for 2020 in place. These include:[68]

> "...build[ing] communities that value and respond to children, young people and parents' demands for safe and well maintained places to play... all children and young people will be able to access world-class play and recreation spaces near where they live."

At the heart of the play strategy is the goal of creating two types of safe places for children to play outside: large, staffed 'adventure' playgrounds costing up to £800,000; and smaller sites costing £20,000 to £50,000. 30 "Pathfinder" LAs will build an adventure playground and build or rennovate several smaller sites while the other 120 "Playbuilder" LAs will just build/renovate the smaller sites. This provision was foreshadowed by £124 million from National Big Lottery Fund for LAs to build play

---

[67]   Private conversation with the authors.

[68]   DCSF & DCMS, *The Play Strategy*, 2008.

areas. The professionalisation of the play workforce was also announced, with funding for 4,000 playworkers to complete a level three vocational qualification.

The central budget for this in 2010/11 is £128 million.[69] In addition to the above public subsidy, the Lottery Fund and the Rowntree Foundation are making substantial contributions to the development of playgrounds. The qualifications industry is also busily training 'playworkers', whose skills are quite different from traditional PE teachers and sports coaches.

Recommendations

These schemes must be considered as expensive luxuries which should be the natural object of interest for the National Lottery (and other charitable organisations). Central funding for new Pathfinder and Playbuilder playgrounds should be suspended. However, where playgrounds are still in the planning stages, sponsors should be required to apply for charitable or LA funding if they wish to continue.

The Playworker qualification is of unproven value and should be suspended immediately.

Estimated impact on central funding

It may be possible to reclaim some of the funding allocated to LAs for 2010-2011 although exactly how much will vary case by case. The capital funding for play facilities was not, to our knowledge, intended to be continued beyond 2011. However the revenue funding of £9 million is likely to be a continuing cost and should be abolished.

---

[69] DCSF, *Play Pathfinder and Playbuilder, Capital and Revenue, Grants: 2010-11*, 2010.

Think Family

On the face of it, there would seem to be a compelling case for giving dysfunctional families more support and counselling. The 'Think Family' agenda consists of measures to train and deploy new parenting advisers, and a Family Intervention Programme designed to reduce anti-social behaviour in problem families.

Its budget in 2010/11 is £65 million.[70] Parent Support Advisors (PSAs), one of the raft of new roles, are funded through the Extended School Sustainability Funding grant mentioned above. The nominal allocation for PSAs is £34.5 million in 2010-2011 but this is non-ringfenced.

None of these measures are innovative. Rather, they merely amplify (or as some have suggested, duplicate) existing services.

The success of programmes such as the KIPP academies in the US and Skill Force in the UK demonstrates what can be done when children's self-esteem is built by honest achievement, rather than mere declaration. West Dunbartonshire has made a major impact by involving parents in their literacy programme – once you understand that your child is not doomed to lead a pointless life, your own life is transfused with purpose.

Recommendations

There is little justification for continuing central subsidy for Think Family programmes. The DCSF evaluation of the Family Intervention Project (FIP) claims to have improved outcomes for target families on a range of measures. However, only 38% of families referred to a FIP completed the intervention with a formal, planned exit. Of those, 32% were still involved in anti-social behaviour. In other words, only 26% of those referred to

---

[70] DCSF, *Approved Think Family 2010-11 Grant Applications: 112 LAs*, 2010.

the FIPs had a recorded positive outcome.[71] There is no recorded data for families which did not formally exit the project. However for the minority of those referred who achieved positive outcomes, the change seems to have been sustained.[72]

Nor do we see any point for government to support the development of a new body of parenting advisers. If any of these new qualifications is of any merit, schools and local authorities should be free to employ people who have them.

Estimated impact on central funding
Abolition would save £65 million a year.

Assessment for Learning & Masters in Teaching and Learning
Assessment for Learning (AfL) is the heart of the "personalised learning agenda", an international movement promoted by some of the world's leading educational theorists.[73] Its effects are only beginning to be felt in England's schools, and this initiative (and the Masters in Teaching and Learning) are designed to accelerate training of heads, teachers and ancillary staff. The AfL budget in 2010/11 was £50 million, while that of the Masters in Teaching and Learning is estimated at a further £15 million.[74]

---

[71] National Centre for Social Research, *ASB Family Intervention Projects Monitoring and Evaluation*, 2010.

[72] Ibid.

[73] This is a complex movement; for an official summary, see the Gilbert Review: http://publications.teachernet.gov.uk/eOrderingDownload/6856-DfES-Teaching%20and%20Learning.pdf

[74] DCSF, *The National Strategies, AfL support and funding for every school*, 2010; the £15 million cost of the Masters in 2010-2011 is based on a two year allocation of £30 million. See www.keele.ac.uk/media/keeleuniversity/fachumsocsci/sclpppp/education/mtl /MTL__Guardian__supplement__lowres.pdf

In terms of pedagogic theory, AfL represents the ultimate development of 'child-centred' education, with each pupil supposedly 'co-authoring' his or her learning objectives. The teacher is then responsible for helping them create their own personalised learning programmes. Serving teachers have described this is a pointless charade; when asked what they want to learn, even the brightest and most motivated pupils merely shrug their shoulders. And how are teachers, who often have to teach more than 200 pupils, supposed to design personalised learning plans for each and every one of them?

Recommendation and estimated impact on central funding
Both programmes should be abolished, saving £65 million a year.

Every Child A Reader (ECAR)

ECAR is a programme designed to provide individual tutoring to six years olds who have not begun to master basic reading skills. While it is clear that urgent action is needed to reduce the appalling number of illiterate children produced by primary schools, Reading Recovery (the main element of ECAR) costs over £6,000 for each successful intervention.[75] By contrast, competing interventions cost as little as £150 per pupil. Southampton officials have estimated that their education budget would have to increase by 50% if every child who qualified for intervention were to receive ECAR.[76] Even then, it would hardly solve the problem: research conducted by the Institute of Education – which is a major stakeholder in Reading Recovery – admits that it does not work with 20% of the pupils enrolled. Independent research in the US and Australia, where

---

[75] T and H Burkard, *Every Child a Reader: An example of how top-down education reforms make matters worse,* Policy Exchange, 2009.

[76] Private conversation with the authors.

Reading Recovery has been used on a large scale, is uniformly negative: gains tend to fade out quickly.

The budget for Reading Recovery (which also includes programmes such as Every Child A Writer and Every Child Counts) is estimated at £56 million in 2010/11.[77] It is widely resented in schools and local authorities where the general feeling is that the money could be put to much better use. It is also completely at odds with the synthetic phonics approach which Tony Blair as Prime Minister and Andrew Adonis as Schools Minister tried to impose upon their reluctant officials. It has frequently been suggested that DfES officials who had previously opposed synthetic phonics demanded ECAR as their price for conceding.

Recommendation and estimated impact on central funding
ECAR should be abolished, saving £56 million a year.

Special Education Needs in the Children's Plan
The Children's Plan set out various government initiatives intended to improve Special Education Needs (SEN) provision. In 2010/11, its budget was £34 million.[78]

Instead of ensuring that all children master the basic spelling code in the first few terms of school, the DCSF now requires teachers to report the developmental level of children who have

---

[77] Estimate based on three year allocation of £169 million. DCSF press notice 2008/0814, *Cutting edge new approach to improve standards in 3Rs*, 2 September 2008.

[78] This comprises Achievement for All (£17 million, DCSF press release 2009/0106, *£200m 'co-location' fund to put schools at the heart of their communities*, 11 June 2009); Cost of SENCO Training (£8.6 million, 2009 SENCO regulations impact assessment); Achievement for All Evaluation and NCSL Support for Schools (£4 million, DCSF Freedom of information response, 24 August 2009); and cost of new ITT and CPD modules from the TDA (£4 million: estimate based on three year budget of £12 millon).

failed. In other words, it is assumed that children have to reach developmental milestones before reading instruction can begin. Specialists will now be trained to recognise ADHD, dyslexia, and other conditions which supposedly explain failure. The old National Literacy Strategy, for all its faults, at least recognised that these were often excuses for inadequate teaching.

The 2008 Regulations set out new requirements for the training and qualification of SEN personnel. However, the value of these qualifications is unproven, and the regulations entail a significant increase in administration.

Recommendation and estimated impact on central funding
Special Education Needs are administered by Local Authorities, not by central government. The inititiatives in the Children's Plan are more likely to hinder Local Authorities and schools than to help. These intitiatives should be dropped. As such it should be abolished, saving £34 million.

Mental Health
The Children's Plan announced an external review of Children and Adolescent Mental Health Services (CAMHS) and a three year pilot of Targeted Mental Health in Schools (TaMHS).[79] The annual budget for TaMHS would be around £27 million if rolled out on a national basis.[80]

This initiative stems from the 1999 DoH study conducted by the Office of National Statistics, which claimed that one out of every

---

[79] CAMHS covers NHS-provided mental health services for children. In general, children are referred to CAMHS by their GP. In contrast, in the words of the DCSF, the purpose of TAMHS is "to enable schools to deliver a holistic, whole school approach to promoting children's mental wellbeing": See www.wmrdc.org.uk/silo/files/annex-a-tamhs-rollout-criteria.doc

[80] This estimate is based on average pilot funding in 2010-2011. See DCSF, *Targeted Mental Health in Schools Grants Circular 2010-2011*, 2010.

ten children suffer from some form of emotional, behavioural or hyperactivity disorder.[81] Clearly, the definition of 'mental disorder' has been stretched. It would be extremely unusual to find that a school with 800 pupils had 80 children with mental health problems, and indeed a miracle if their teachers could cope.

TaMHS trains teachers to be, in effect, low level child psychiatrists. This is yet another burden which teachers could well do without. A psychiatrist should be impartial – not a person who deals with the subject every day and who may be prejudiced by their past interactions with them. TaMHS also places mental health professionals within schools, effectively trawling for business.

While young people who suffer from real mental health problems definitely do need help (and can get such help through CAMHS), it should be recognised that this is ultimately a problem for the child and its parents. While some teachers may welcome training in recognising signs of mental disturbance in one of their pupils, few would relish the added responsibilities that come from the extension of their role to include 'pre-emptive psychiatry'. And nor should they; it should not be the role of a school to send a child off for psychiatric evaluation because a child is inattentive during class – informing parents of their concerns should be enough. Still less is it the role of the teacher to act as an amateur therapist. Nor is it necessarily sound public policy to encourage a 'counselling culture' which can foster a self-obsessed, excuse-seeking mindset.

In contrast, CAMHS is often underfunded and oversubscribed. In 2007 Hertfordshire CAMHS could only cut waiting lists by raising

---

[81] Meltzer et al, *The mental health of children and adolescents in Great Britain*, Office for National Statistics. 2000.

the thresholds to access the service, which meant that some parents and children seeking help were denied it.[82] This is a perverse approach to mental health – denying help to those who are seeking it, while actively seeking new cases. Public services should respond to the needs of taxpayers, rather than pursuing their own agenda.

Recommendation and estimated impact on central funding
TaMHS is misconceived and has potentially denied resources to CaMHS. This would save £27 million relative to a national roll-out of the programme. Funding for CaMHS should continue, if not be enhanced.

Safe at Home
The Safe At Home scheme (with a £9 million budget in 2010-11) entails the provision of home safety equipment – such as stairwell and fire guards, non-slip bath mats – to homes of infants from birth to the age of five from disadvantaged families.[83] The average set is estimated to retail for an average of around £60. After the child(ren) reach their fifth birthday, the parents are required to surrender the equipment in good order.

Well-meaning as this scheme may be, the idea that the equipment will be retrieved and reused after five years is somewhat optimistic. The smaller equipment would cost far less to replace than it would to retrieve; a set of corner cushions

---

[82] In 2007, Hertfordshire Children's Services Authority Area *Joint Area Review* stated that: "Waiting lists for CAMHS have been long and, although these have recently been reduced, this has been achieved by raising the thresholds to access the service, rather than by extending provision, leading to some children being denied access to the service. Early access to CAMHS remains poor for children and young people with less complex needs."

[83] Funding is provided by a monthly grant from the DCSF, but the annual cost is estimated from two year allocation of £18 million.

retails for around 85p. As for more expensive equipment; if fitting wall mounted stair guards and window restrictors requires a CRB checked, qualified craft person then removing them will require the same. By the time this equipment has been cleaned, safety checked and reinstalled (by a CRB checked, qualified craft person) the costs will probably have far exceeded the cost of buying a new set.

All of this is assuming that after five years the equipment is still there and in working order. People move house, equipment gets broken, loaned, given or thrown away.

Recommendation and estimated impact on central funding
Central funding should be withdrawn from this scheme. Those local authorities who wished to continue with this scheme would be free to use their own funds to pay for it. Charities and voluntary organisations should also be encouraged to provide help in this area (as they were doing before the introduction of this programme).

6. CONCLUSION

It must be emphasised that the aims behind most of the programmes in the Children's Plan are laudable. We all want to see all families – particularly the most disadvantaged – have the best possible start in life. What is in dispute, however, is whether the Children's Plan can achieve such goals.

Underlying these programmes is a remarkable confidence in the ability of the state to regulate the lives of its citizens and to control their destinies. This confidence appears to be misplaced for it is hard to find much benefit from many of the programmes (the weakness of many of the programme evaluations is also to be condemned). The centralised approach, where a Whitehall department creates and funds an endless stream of new programmes, is a model which must now be questioned.

But it is not just that these programmes are ineffective. They can also be damaging: they tend to undermine front line services, chipping away at teachers' and social workers' professionalism and inititiative; they are highly bureaucratic, creating extraordinary levels of management; and they often fail to focus on those families who are most in need.

And of course they are expensive.

Spending more is not the answer. The Labour Party was right when it recognised in its 1997 Manifesto that: "The myth that the solution to every problem is increased spending has been comprehensively dispelled." Now is the time to turn that sentiment into action.

For a more effective – and incidentally, far cheaper – alternative would be to devolve as much as possible, as far down as possible: responsibility for these initiatives should in most cases be passed to parents, to professionals, to schools and to local authorities. Help should be focused on those families who are most in need. They will benefit most from intensive support programmes such as that pioneered by Westminster Council's Family Recovery Programme.[84] That approach will have a far more realistic chance of meeting the original aims of the Children's Plan.

---

[84] For more details on Westminster Council's approach, see Colin Barrow et al, *A Magna Carta for Localism: Three practical steps to make localism real*, Centre for Policy Studies, March 2010.

ANNEX A

PROGRAMMES IN THE CHILDREN'S PLAN

Programme	Stream	2010-2011 Budget (million)	Source
Anti-Social Behaviour			
	Acceptable Behaviour Contracts	£7	1
	Challenge and Support Projects	£4	2
Aiming High for Disabled Children			
	Short Break Services revenue	£178	3
	Transition Support Programme	£15	3
	Individual Budget Pilots	£1	3
	Short Break Services Capital	£52	3
	DCATCH	£13	3
	Family Fund	£26	4
	AHDC Pallative Care Funding	£10	5
	DoH Funding to PCTs	£103	6
	Subtotal Revenue	£346	
	Subtotal Capital	£52	
	Total	**£398**	
Asessment for Learning			
	Assessment for Learning	£50	7

Bercow Review of Services for Children with Speech, Language and Communication Needs

Becta grants to the Alternative and Augmentive Communications sector	£1	8
Communication Champion, Communication Secretariat, communication review in 2010 and National Year of Speech, Language and Communication	£1	8
Research programme	£1	8
Children, Young People and Families grants	£0	8
Commissioning Pathfinders and Framework and Community Equipment Model Development	£3	8
Total	**£5**	

Childcare

Sufficiency and Access	£129	3
Every Child a Talker	£17	3
Childcare Capital (SSEYCG)	£214	3
Child care for 2 year olds	£67	3
Extending childcare for 3-4 year olds	£340	10
Subtotal Revenue	£553	
Subtotal Capital	£214	
Total	**£767**	

Child Safety

Safe at Home	£9	11
Funding to Childline	£8	12
Child death review process funding	£8	13
Total	**£25**	

Change 4 Life

"Evidence based marketing policy" aimed at reducing obesity	£25	14

Do it 4 Real

Do it 4 Real: 10-16 holidays/camps	£7	15

Early Years Foundation Stage

Graduate Leader Fund (Local Grants)	£99	3
Graduate Leader Fund (CWDC Funding)	£27	3
Buddying Pilots	£5	3
0-7 Partnerships	£3	3
Early Years, Outcomes, Quality and Inclusion	£164	3
Total	**£298**	

ECAR et al

Every Child a Reader, Every Child Counts and Every Child a Writer	£56

Extended Schools

Extended Schools Start up	£71	9
Extended Schools Sustainability Funding	£190	8
Extended Schools Subsidy	£167	8
Extended Schools Capital Funding	£46	16
Extended Schools: Acedemic Focused Study Support	£33	16
Subtotal Revenue	£461	
Subtotal Capital	£46	
Total	**£507**	

Family Learning

Family Learning Impact Funding	£10	17

Family Pathfinders

Family Pathfinders and Young Carers	£5	18

Find Your Talent

Find Your Talent Pathfinders	£8	19

Food in Schools

Raising FSM threshold	£140	20
School meal subsidy	£79	10
School Food Trust Funding	£8	21
School kitchen capital funding	£50	24

FSM Pilots	£10	23
FSM Pilots (PBR 2009)	£35	20
Food Tech ingredients for FSM pupils	£3	22
Subtotal Revenue	£275	
Subtotal Capital	£50	
Total	**£325**	

Masters in Teaching and learning

Masters in Teaching and learning	£15	25

Mental Health

Targeted Mental health in Schools	£28	26

National Challenge

National Challenge	£217	27

Neet provision

Entry 2 Learning	Unknown - up to £22	28

Overcrowding pilots

Overcrowding pilots	£5	29

PE

PE and Sports Strategy for Young People	£191	10, 30, 31

The Play Strategy

Play Funding	£128	32

School Exclusion

Alternative Provision pilots	£9	1

Social Work

Social Work Practice Pilots	£3	40

Special Educational Needs

Achievement for All	£17	34
SENCO Training	£9	35
One-to-one tuition	£0	
Achievement for All Evaluation and NCSL Support for schools	£4	34
New ITT and CPD modules from TDA**	£4	36
Partnership for Literacy	£0	
Total	**£34**	

Sure Start

Children's Centre Revenue Funding (SSEYCG)	£883	3
Sure Start Local Programmes Revenue Funding (SSEYCG)	£252	3
Sure Start Capital Funding (GSSG)	£315	9
Children's Centre Capital Funding SSEYCG)	£101	3
Subtotal Revenue	£1,135	
Subtotal Capital	£416	
Total	**£1,551**	

Think family

Think Family	£64	6

Young Offenders

Expanding resettlement provision for children leaving custody	£2	38
Targeting young offenders	£22	39

Youth Provision

Positive Activities for Young People (PAYP)	£95	13
Youth opportunity fund	£41	37
Youth capital fund	£26	37
Myplace Funding	£31	36
Subtotal Revenue	£136	
Subtotal Capital	£57	
Total	**£193**	

GRAND TOTAL	**£4,959**	

Sources

1   Estimate based on one third of three year budget of £15 million, DCSF, 2007, The Children's Plan, page 125: http://www.dcsf.gov.uk/childrensplan/

2   DCSF, 2010, Challenge and Support Project Grant 2010-2011:
http://www.dcsf.gov.uk/everychildmatters/news-and-communications/local-authority-circulars-2008-2011/lac2402100005/

3   DCSF, 2010, Sure Start and Early Years Childcare Grant and Aiming High for Disabled Children Allocations 2008-2011:
http://www.dcsf.gov.uk/everychildmatters/research/publications/surestartpublications/1925/

4   DCSF Press notice 2007/0234, December 2007, £53M to help diabled children, young people and their families:
http://www.dcsf.gov.uk/pns/DisplayPN.cgi?pn__id=2007__0234

5   Half of 2 year budget of £20 million:
http://www.dcsf.gov.uk/everychildmatters/healthandwellbeing/ahdc/palliativecare/palliativecare/

6   Health lives, Brighter Futures:
http://www.dh.gov.uk/prod__consum__dh/groups/dh__digitalassets/documents/digitalasset/dh__094397.pdf

7   AfL e-bulletin: Spring 2010:
http://nationalstrategies.standards.dcsf.gov.uk/node/348695?uc%20=%20force__uj

8   DCSF and DH, 2008, Better Communication:
http://www.dcsf.gov.uk/slcnaction/downloads/Better__Communication__Final.pdf

9   DCSF, 2010, Area Based Grant Allocations 2010-2011:
http://www.teachernet.gov.uk/docbank/index.cfm?id=12227

10   DCSF, 2010, Standards Fund Allocations 2008-2011:
http://www.teachernet.gov.uk/docbank/index.cfm?id=12227

11   Estimate based on half of £18 million 2 year allocation - DCSF Press notice 009/0036, February 2009,Children's minister: £18 million to help keep children 'safe at home': http://www.dcsf.gov.uk/pns/DisplayPN.cgi?pn__id=2009__0036

12   Estimate based on a quarter of four year allocation of £30 million - DCSF, 2007, The Children's Plan, page 48: http://www.dcsf.gov.uk/childrensplan/

13   DCSF, 2008, Children's Services Funding Worksheet 2008-2011:
http://www.dcsf.gov.uk/everychildmatters/__download/?id=1924

14   Estimate based on one third of three year budget of £75 million - DH, 2008, Healthy Weight, Healthy Lives:
http://webarchive.nationalarchives.gov.uk/+/www.dh.gov.uk/en/publichealth/healthimprovement/obesity/dh__082383

15   House of Commons Written Answers, 22 March 2010, Column 92W:
http://www.publications.parliament.uk/pa/cm200910/cmhansrd/cm100322/text/100322w0019.htm

16 DCSF, 2008, FUNDING EXTENDED SCHOOLS: DCSF guidance for local authorities and schools: http://www.teachernet.gov.uk/docbank/index.cfm?id=12859

17 House of Commons Written Answers, Hansard 22 Feb 2010 : Column 306W: http://www.publications.parliament.uk/pa/cm200910/cmhansrd/cm100222/text/100222 w0066.htm

18 Cabinet Office press release 4th May 2008, 15 local areas to lead Pathfinder projects supporting vulnerable families : http://webarchive.nationalarchives.gov.uk/20100202100434/http://www.cabinetoffice.g ov.uk/social_exclusion_task_force/news/2008/080504_15_local_areas.aspx

19 Estimate based on one third of three year budget of £25 million - DCMS, 2009, Lifting People, Lifting Places pg 11: http://webarchive.nationalarchives.gov.uk/+/http://www.culture.gov.uk/images/publicat ions/Lifting_People.pdf

20 HM Treasury, 2009 Pre Budget Report: http://webarchive.nationalarchives.gov.uk/+/http://www.hm-treasury.gov.uk/prebud_pbr09_repindex.htm

21 Stamford, 26th May 2010, Government Slashes School food Trust's budget by £1m, Caterersearch.com news: http://www.caterersearch.com/Articles/2010/05/26/333515/government-slashes-school-food-trusts-budget-by-1m.htm

22 DCSF press notice 2008/0015, 22nd January 2008, Compulsary cooking lessons for all young people: http://www.dcsf.gov.uk/pns/DisplayPN.cgi?pn_id=2008_0015

23 Estimate based on half of two year budget of £20 million - DCSF press notice 2008/0212, 24th September 2008, New £20m free school meals pilot: http://www.dcsf.gov.uk/pns/DisplayPN.cgi?pn_id=2008_0212

24 Estimate based on half of 2 year budget of £100 million - School Food Trust, Targeted Capital Fund for kitchens and dining rooms: http://www.schoolfoodtrust.org.uk/UploadDocs/Library/Documents/capital_fund_for _kitchens&dining_rooms.pdf

25 Estimate based on half of 2 year budget of £30 million - Hoare, 2010, Masters of the Classroom, Education Guardian: www.keele.ac.uk/media/keeleuniversity/fachumsocsci/sclpppp/education/mtl /MTL_Guardian_supplement_lowres.pdf

26 DCSF, 2010, Targeted Mental health in Schools Grant 2010-2011: http://www.dcsf.gov.uk/everychildmatters/news-and-communications/local-authority-circulars-2008-2011/lac2203100001/

27 Freedom of Information response from the DCSF, 29 April 2010

28 Funding could be as much as £21.5 million. Revealing the future cost of the Entry 2 Learning project was deemed not to be in the public interest by the project manager: Freedom of Information Response from DCSF, 30th September 2009

29 Estimate based on one third of three year budget of £15 million - Communities and Local Government, 2007, Tackling Overcrowding in England an Action Plan, pg 7: http://www.communities.gov.uk/documents/housing/pdf/10.pdf

30   Estimate based on previous years' funding: Freedom of Information Response from DCSF, 13 May 2010

31   Estimate based on previous year's funding - House of Commons Written Answers, Hansard, 9th June 2009: http://services.parliament.uk/hansard/Commons/ByDate/20090609/writtenanswers/part009.html

32   DCSF, 2010, Play Pathfinder and Playbuilder Grants: http://www.dcsf.gov.uk/everychildmatters/news-and-communications/local-authority-circulars-2008-2011/lac2502100003/

33   Estimate based on one third of three year budget of £26.5 million, DCSF, 2007, The Children's Plan, pg.84: http://www.dcsf.gov.uk/childrensplan/

34   Freedom of Information response from the DCSF, 1st September 2009

35   DCSF, 2009, Expalnatory memorandum to the Education (Special Educational Needs Co-ordinators) (England) (Amendment) Regulations 2009: http://www.governornet.co.uk/linkAttachments/memo%20senco%202009.pdf

36   DCSF press notice 2009/0256, 16th December 2009, £31m to build new youth facilities in the most deprived areas: http://www.dcsf.gov.uk/pns/DisplayPN.cgi?pn_id=2009_0256

37   DCSF, 2010, Youth Opportunity Fund and Youth Capital Funds Grants 2010-2011: http://www.dcsf.gov.uk/everychildmatters/news-and-communications/local-authority-circulars-2008-2011/lac2901100006/

38   Estimate based on one third of 3 year budget of £6 million: HM Government, 2008, Youth Crime Action Plan

39   Estimate based on one third of three year budget of £66 million: DCSF, 2007, The Children's Plan, page 125: http://www.dcsf.gov.uk/childrensplan/

40   Estimate based on previous year's funding: McGregor, 4th March 2010, Union members may boycott Sandwell looked-after children pilot, communitycare.co.uk: http://www.communitycare.co.uk/Articles/2010/03/04/113955/unison-threatens-to-scupper-sandwell-practice-pilot.htm

BECOME AN ASSOCIATE OF
THE CENTRE FOR POLICY STUDIES

The Centre for Policy Studies is one of Britain's best-known and most respected think tanks. Independent from all political parties and pressure groups, it consistently advocates a distinctive case for smaller, less intrusive government, with greater freedom and responsibility for individuals, families, business and the voluntary sector.

Through our Associate Membership scheme, we welcome supporters who take an interest in our work. Associate Membership is available for £100 a year (or £90 a year if paid by bankers' order). Becoming an Associate will entitle you to:

- all CPS publications produced in a 12-month period
- invitations to lectures and conferences
- advance notice by e-mail of our publications, briefing papers and invitations to special events

For more details, please write or telephone to:
The Secretary
Centre for Policy Studies
57 Tufton Street, London SW1P 3QL
Tel: 020 7222 4488
Fax: 020 7222 4388
e-mail: mail@cps.org.uk
Website: www.cps.org.uk

SOME RECENT PUBLICATIONS

An end to factory schools by Anthony Seldon
"Our schools turn out unemployable blockheads" – Cristina Odone, The Daily Telegraph

A Magna Carta for Localism by Colin Barrow, Stephen Greenhalgh and Edward Lister
"A report by three men who have proven credentials in achieving just such a formula for their local communities which is now so desperately needed on a national level" – ConservativeHome

School Quangos: a blueprint for abolition and reform by Tom Burkard and Sam Talbot Rice
"More autonomy and fewer quangos: think tank earmarks £633 million savings" – headline in *Times Educational Supplement*

Wasted: the betrayal of white working class and black Caribbean boys by Harriet Sergeant
'I cannot remember when I last read something which inspired such exasperation, hopelessness and rage" – Bruce Anderson, *The Independent*